RESTART DEVOTIONAL

Rediscovering God's Plan For Your Life

Bruce Johnson, Jr.

Copyright © 2024 by Bruce Johnson, Jr.

All rights reserved. This book or any portion thereof may not be reproduced or used in any manner whatsoever without the express written permission of the publisher except for the use of brief quotations in a book review.

Printed in the United States of America

First Edition, 2024

PAPERBACK ISBN: 979-8-8692-5345-3

HARDBACK ISBN: 979-8-8692-7855-5

EBOOK ISBN: 979-8-8692-7854-8

Red Pen Edits and Consulting

www.redpeneditsllc.com

Contents

Day 1: Connecting with God — 1

Day 2: It's Already In You — 5

Day 3: It Is Time To Live! — 9

Day 4: In The Face Of God — 13

Day 5: Gold Is On The Menu — 17

Day 6: Covered — 21

Day 7: Public Success, Private Failure — 25

Day 8: It's Just The Season — 29

Day 9: Pretty Hurts — 33

Day 10: Strong Desires — 37

Day 11: Arrogant Worship — 41

Day 12: You Know You're Tired — 45

Day 13: Eat Up — 49

Day 14: Anoint My Head With Oil — 53

Day 15: The Right King — 57

Day 16: Waiting On God — 61

Day 17: Strength For The Journey — 63

Day 18: Walk By Faith — 67

Day 19: It's Only A Matter Of Time — 71

Day 20: A Reason To Continue — 75

Day 21: A New Man	77
Day 22: Anything Is Possible	81
Day 23: Are You Ready To Turn?	83
Day 24: Be Not Weary	87
Day 25: Never Forget	89
Day 26: Your True Identity	91
Day 27: It Is You!	93
Day 28: Unending Worship	97
Day 29: Why Come Down?	99
Day 30: Make This A Habit	101
Resources	104
About The Author	105

Dedications

I would like to dedicate this devotional to the memory of my late mother, **Patrice Lavern Johnson**, whose passion for writing I hope to continue on.

I also dedicate this devotional to my Haitian Queen, **Soraya**, and my Haitian Princesses, **Mckenzie and Averi**.

Day 1

Connecting with God

1 Samuel 3:1-10 NIV

The boy Samuel ministered before the Lord under Eli. In those days the word of the Lord was rare; there were not many visions.

² One night Eli, whose eyes were becoming so weak that he could barely see, was lying down in his usual place. ³ The lamp of God had not yet gone out, and Samuel was lying down in the house of the Lord, where the ark of God was. ⁴ Then the Lord called Samuel.

Samuel answered, "Here I am." ⁵ And he ran to Eli and said, "Here I am; you called me."

But Eli said, "I did not call; go back and lie down." So he went and lay down.

⁶ Again the Lord called, "Samuel!" And Samuel got up and went to Eli and said, "Here I am; you called me."

"My son," Eli said, "I did not call; go back and lie down."

⁷ Now Samuel did not yet know the Lord: The word of the Lord had not yet been revealed to him.

⁸ A third time the Lord called, "Samuel!" And Samuel got up and went to Eli and said, "Here I am; you called me."

Then Eli realized that the Lord was calling the boy. ⁹ So Eli told Samuel, "Go and lie down, and if he calls you, say, 'Speak, Lord, for your servant is listening.'" So Samuel went and lay down in his place.

¹⁰ The Lord came and stood there, calling as at the other times, "Samuel! Samuel!" Then Samuel said, "Speak, for your servant is listening."

I'll never forget the day I was so low in my mind while traveling with my Bishop. I was present in body, but my spirit was somewhere else. During the altar call, my Pastor noticed everyone was crying out to God except me. He walked away from the altar, over to the musician's pit, and said to me 'Open your mouth, this is for you too'. Wow, what a revelation. As musicians and singers, we are often plagued with the idea that what we do only benefits those we are ministering to or accompanying. This is a huge misconception that I hope to confront in this devotional because we are missing out on an important piece of what we do as worship leaders. Now when I say worship leaders, I mean it in an all-inclusive sense - meaning whatever part you play in the worship service, you are leading the people in worship to God.

Today's scripture talks about a young man by the name of Samuel who has been serving the prophet Eli since he was a child, which most of us can relate to. During this time in Israel, God's voice was very rare - what a sad thing to experience but I am often wondering, was the issue the silence of God or the sin in Israel was so loud it drowned out the voice of God. Let me explain. Eli was the priest during this time and even though he was a righteous man, his sons, Hophni and Phinehas were defiling the temple with their lustful actions. Not only a lust for women but a lust for power. Due to their actions in the temple, and Eli's decision to turn a blind eye, God kills both sons which leaves the legacy of Eli hanging in the balance. One day while he is asleep, God calls Samuel by name. Twice he runs to Eli thinking it was his voice but Eli lets him know that it was God and the next time he hears his name, to respond, 'speak Lord, for thy servant hears you'.

This is the major point I want you to grab today.

Even in the midst of you serving the people, God desires to speak to you, and in the right time, he desires to speak through you. This can come through your playing, your singing, and even your dancing. These are all ways that God gets his messages to us. With this being noted, ask God to speak to you as you are His servant. I challenge you to get still in God's presence, talk to Him, and spend time in quietness, and listen for His voice. Lastly, give yourself time. As you are building this connection with God, do not get discouraged if you do not hear Him audibly. You can have a feeling or a thought you did not conjure up. It may even be something as simple as a feeling of peace coming over you. Whatever your experience is, believe that it is God connecting back with you.

Let's get ready for a day connected with God!

In what ways does this thought make me want to **RESTART**?

_____
_____
_____
_____
_____
_____
_____
_____
_____
_____

What steps am I willing to take today to **RESTART**?

1. _____
   _____
   _____

2. _____
   _____
   _____

3. _____
   _____
   _____

Day 2

It's Already In You

> Genesis 1:11 NIV
> "Then God said, "Let the land produce vegetation: seed-bearing plants and trees on the land that bear fruit with seed in it, according to their various kinds." And it was so.

What kind of confidence would you have today if I told you that everything you need for your success lies on the inside of you? What if I told you that just like the trees in today's scripture, God placed the ability to produce exactly what you were called to produce on the inside of you? This is liberating in the fact that we often look for the right connection, the right gig, or the right viral video to set us up for success, but all of those things we search for are only meant to complement and enhance what we already have ourselves.

I remember stressing myself out trying to figure out who I needed to connect with in order to play for certain artists. As I look back retrospectively most of the opportunities I had, came to me because I was spirit-led, well-prepared, and professional. I worked on my craft. I practiced and I prayed for God to maximize my abilities. What you house on the inside of you is sitting there waiting to be crafted and matured by nobody but you. The mind-blowing part of all of this is that even at your current level of skill and ability, you have barely scratched the surface. You must never forget that it is God who has given you His characteristics, which is foremost creativity. Therefore, you must seek Him to find your highest level of creativity.

Now go!

Begin to seek God's spirit in your life in order to take on His characteristics and even the sky is not the limit to what you can create.

My prayer for you today is that you get still for a few minutes and ask God for His spirit before you go about your day and expect your spirit to be ignited.

Let's get ready for a day in the spirit!

In what ways does this thought make me want to **RESTART**?

___

What steps am I willing to take today to **RESTART**?

1. ___

2. ___

3. ___

Day 3

It Is Time To Live!

> Genesis 3:1-7 NIV
>
> Now the serpent was more crafty than any of the wild animals the Lord God had made. He said to the woman, "Did God really say, 'You must not eat from any tree in the garden'?"
>
> ² The woman said to the serpent, "We may eat fruit from the trees in the garden, ³ but God did say, 'You must not eat fruit from the tree that is in the middle of the garden, and you must not touch it, or you will die.'"
>
> ⁴ "You will not certainly die," the serpent said to the woman. ⁵ "For God knows that when you eat from it your eyes will be opened, and you will be like God, knowing good and evil."
>
> ⁶ When the woman saw that the fruit of the tree was good for food and pleasing to the eye, and also desirable for gaining wisdom, she took some and ate it. She also gave some to her husband, who was with her, and he ate it. ⁷ Then the eyes of both of them were opened, and they realized they were naked; so they sewed fig leaves together and made coverings for themselves.

My wife has the annoying tendency to 'find God' in Disney movies. Don't ask. Just keep reading. I seem to have picked up her mantle as I was praying about today's devotion and thought about a story we all know about a wooden puppet named,... come on say it... Pinocchio. Now before you start laughing, this is a devotional so get serious. He was created by a man named Geppetto, and for a while his creator enjoyed what he looked like but there was a problem. In order for Pinocchio to serve his purpose in Geppetto's life, he needed something... life. Now if I have not lost you completely, a fairy comes along and at his request, life comes to Pinocchio and he is able to fulfill his purpose in his creator's desire.

Many of us are going through life, traveling the roads, getting paid, getting views, serving in our local Churches, but if we can be honest... something is missing. You see, God takes no pleasure in us operating outside of what He has called us to do, and even though the money and comments are satisfying, that emptiness you still feel is because you have yet to tap into the desire of your creator. No more existing for the approval of others - it's time to live. How does this happen? You need the breath of God to breathe on you and the truth is, he already has, but have you realized it and accepted it? We know what it's like to move a crowd, but do we know what it's like to change someone's life? We know what it's like to stir up a service and we have learned the art of flowing, but when have you ever gotten so connected with the spirit while playing that you felt yourself getting caught up to the point that you can't play anymore?

Adam was created to fulfill a God assignment, as you have, but he could not be effective in what he was doing as long as he was just existing. There was another step in the process. God breathed His breath giving Adam his spirit and ability.

My prayer for you today is that you desire to no longer just live as usual, but that you ask God to breathe on you again. This time, when He breathes on you, you will operate in His ability. You will be limitless in what you can accomplish, and you will feel the impact along with those you minister to.

Let today be a day of new life!

In what ways does this thought make me want to **RESTART**?

___

What steps am I willing to take today to **RESTART**?

1. ___

2. ___

3. ___

Day 4

In The Face Of God

> Exodus 33:12-23 NIV
>
> [12] Moses said to the Lord, "You have been telling me, 'Lead these people,' but you have not let me know whom you will send with me. You have said, 'I know you by name and you have found favor with me.' [13] If you are pleased with me, teach me your ways so I may know you and continue to find favor with you. Remember that this nation is your people."
>
> [14] The Lord replied, "My Presence will go with you, and I will give you rest."
>
> [15] Then Moses said to him, "If your Presence does not go with us, do not send us up from here. [16] How will anyone know that you are pleased with me and with your people unless you go with us? What else will distinguish me and your people from all the other people on the face of the earth?"
>
> [17] And the Lord said to Moses, "I will do the very thing you have asked, because I am pleased with you and I know you by name."
>
> [18] Then Moses said, "Now show me your glory."
>
> [19] And the Lord said, "I will cause all my goodness to pass in front of you, and I will proclaim my name, the Lord, in your presence. I will have mercy on whom I will have mercy, and I will have compassion on whom I will have compassion. [20] But," he said, "you cannot see my face, for no one may see me and live."
>
> [21] Then the Lord said, "There is a place near me where you may stand on a rock. [22] When my glory passes by, I will put you in a cleft in the rock and cover you with my hand until I have passed by. [23] Then I will remove my hand and you will see my back; but my face must not be seen."

God has chosen a special man by the name of Moses to lead his people Israel out of bondage in Egypt into Canaan which is the promised land. Oftentimes, as a leader, Moses shows us that in order to lead

God's people, you need his guidance the whole way. This scripture is one of those cases where he desired, more than guidance, to see the face of God.

There are moments in life when you realize God's presence is not enough in your life. There must be more to this - going from just feeling God to experiencing God's glory. He is asking for a deeper understanding of God, not just a feeling but a knowing through revelation. What kind of worship would you offer God if you saw him physically? Imagine this and to Moses' temporary disappointment, God says 'You cannot see my face, for no man can see my face and live.' How anticlimactic is it for God not to grant your request of wanting more of Him? But God and Moses teach us a strong lesson here. What God does say is, ' I have a place by me…and when I pass by you I will put you in the cleft of a rock, and once I pass by I will take my hand away and you will see my back'. This experience changed Moses' life forever which poses a question.

Are you satisfied with seeing any part of God that He desires to show you?

Shouldn't any part of God be enough for you?

Or are you still that controlling of your relationship with Him that He must meet every desire exactly how you want?

It takes maturity to realize that any part of God is the glory of God! If it is His hand you see, that is His glory. If He shows you His eye, that is His glory. Even if it is His foot you see, that is His glory!

My prayer for you today is that you become content and honored to be able to behold any part of God. Let your prayer today be that of Moses, 'I pray you, show me your glory!"

In what ways does this thought make me want to **RESTART**?

_____
_____
_____
_____
_____
_____
_____
_____
_____
_____

What steps am I willing to take today to **RESTART**?

1. _____
   _____
   _____

2. _____
   _____
   _____

3. _____
   _____
   _____

Day 5

Gold Is On The Menu

> Exodus 32:1-10 NIV
>
> When the people saw that Moses was so long in coming down from the mountain, they gathered around Aaron and said, "Come, make us gods[a] who will go before us. As for this fellow Moses who brought us up out of Egypt, we don't know what has happened to him."
>
> 2 Aaron answered them, "Take off the gold earrings that your wives, your sons and your daughters are wearing, and bring them to me." 3 So all the people took off their earrings and brought them to Aaron. 4 He took what they handed him and made it into an idol cast in the shape of a calf, fashioning it with a tool. Then they said, "These are your gods,[b] Israel, who brought you up out of Egypt."
>
> 5 When Aaron saw this, he built an altar in front of the calf and announced, "Tomorrow there will be a festival to the Lord." 6 So the next day the people rose early and sacrificed burnt offerings and presented fellowship offerings. Afterward they sat down to eat and drink and got up to indulge in revelry.
>
> 7 Then the Lord said to Moses, "Go down, because your people, whom you brought up out of Egypt, have become corrupt. 8 They have been quick to turn away from what I commanded them and have made themselves an idol cast in the shape of a calf. They have bowed down to it and sacrificed to it and have said, 'These are your gods, Israel, who brought you up out of Egypt.'
>
> 9 "I have seen these people," the Lord said to Moses, "and they are a stiff-necked people. 10 Now leave me alone so that my anger may burn against them and that I may destroy them. Then I will make you into a great nation."

We as humans desire worship, but what can be dangerous is when our worship is unbiased toward the God of the Bible. Oh! You know what I mean. We worship our gifts when we go to minister without praying first. We worship our cars. We worship our partners. We worship our money, and it all shows in our dedication to them versus our dedication to the things of God which speaks to our dedication to God himself. But all is not lost. This is what our scripture warns us of.

The children of Israel were brought out of Egypt to worship God in the wilderness as they journeyed to Canaan which is the promised land. Moses went up to Mt. Sinai to receive what we now know to be the 10 commandments, but apparently, he is up there too long for the followers. They get anxious and turn to Aaron who is second in command and force him to make them something to worship. He takes all of the gold they have and creates a golden calf, and they make the announcement. "This is your God, O Israel, who brought you up from the land of Egypt." I have two problems with this.

#1. As a leader, never drop your standard to accommodate the anxiety of the people.

Moving on.

#2. Worship does not go down. Worship only goes up. We worship God as our creator. He does not worship us for being created. Therefore, how did they fathom they could create something and worship it? This is rooted in the teachings they received in Egypt where they worshipped everything as a God, but this was never taught by Moses to be true.

I'll cut through the field a bit. As their punishment, Moses burned the golden calf, ground it into powder, and made them drink it.

My intention this morning is to make you grateful that God did not allow you to be consumed by the things in life you have put in His place out of His jealousy towards us. We have been given grace to where he gives us chance after chance to cast down the idols that we have erected in our lives.

Take time today to be thankful that you were not consumed by what you consumed!

In what ways does this thought make me want to **RESTART**?

_____
_____
_____
_____
_____
_____
_____
_____
_____
_____

What steps am I willing to take today to **RESTART**?

1. _____
_____
_____

2. _____
_____
_____

3. _____
_____
_____

Day 6

Covered

> Psalm 3:1-8 NIV
>
> 1 Lord, how many are my foes!
> How many rise up against me!
> 2 Many are saying of me,
> "God will not deliver him."[b]
> 3 But you, Lord, are a shield around me,
> my glory, the One who lifts my head high.
> 4 I call out to the Lord,
> and he answers me from his holy mountain.
> 5 I lie down and sleep;
> I wake again, because the Lord sustains me.
> 6 I will not fear though tens of thousands
> assail me on every side.
> 7 Arise, Lord!
> Deliver me, my God!
> Strike all my enemies on the jaw;
> break the teeth of the wicked.
> 8 From the Lord comes deliverance.
> May your blessing be on your people.

I love the transparency of David as a writer, but to be honest, his writing ability comes from his ability to be transparent. Have you ever read something or heard someone speaking and could tell it was coming from a second-hand experience? David was not that guy. In fact, there were some things he wrote that would have him locked up in the times we are living in now, but we thank God for statutes of limitations.

In life, we incur enemies. Some are unwarranted. Some we have brought upon ourselves, and sometimes we are our own enemy. Nonetheless, enemies are in our lives whether we like it or not. It is the constant war between good and evil. And as you go through life, your enemies go deeper into your conscience without your permission. These enemies now become fear, doubt, anger, lust, pride, shame - add your own as you see fit. These are the enemies that hinder us from progressing in life and keep us at a standstill in our relationship with God. We have missed years of production and progression while being controlled by these enemies and it has taken up space that we originally designated for God. Verse 2 sums up the intent behind these enemies by taunting David that there is no deliverance for him in God.

You must take courage that God is your shield. Now most of the time when we think of a shield, we are thinking of a warrior with a heavy iron shield in front of him, but that's the beauty of our God. The shield he is to us covers our entire being - physically and spiritually. This means there are no points at which the enemy has an entry point to get to you - even in your mind. Everything we do is by faith and confession. You must believe and confess over yourself against those enemies in your mind, that your mind is shielded by God and the enemy no longer has an entry point into your thoughts. Will the thoughts go away immediately? Absolutely not! But with daily confession over yourself, you will see that the weapons in your mind form, but they will never prosper.

My prayer over you today is that you begin to have faith and confess victory in your mind for the rest of your days, starting today!

In what ways does this thought make me want to **RESTART**?

_____
_____
_____
_____
_____
_____
_____
_____
_____
_____

What steps am I willing to take today to **RESTART**?

1. _____
_____
_____

2. _____
_____
_____

3. _____
_____
_____

Day 7

Public Success, Private Failure

> 2 Kings 5:1 NIV
>
> Now Naaman was commander of the army of the king of Aram. He was a great man in the sight of his master and highly regarded, because through him the Lord had given victory to Aram. He was a valiant soldier, but he had leprosy.

Father, husband, brother, man of God, jack of all trades.

These are just a few of the names we are given as men by individuals on the outside. But how does this list sound?

Inconsistent, weed head, womanizer, quitter, freeloader, dead beat.

Now these are some of the labels we see when we think of ourselves. The question is, who's telling the truth?

Naaman is a perfect example of us as men who have multiple responsibilities and many lives depending on us. He had won many victories, so he was superb at his job. He worked his way up the chain of command from being an entry-level soldier to the captain of the whole army. He has honor among his own people and even God inspired the writer to deem him as a "mighty man of valor". This sounds like a guy we need to pattern ourselves after, right? Not so fast.

We see his greatest attributes laid out so nicely and then we are blindsided by some unforeseen and seemingly contradictory information. He's a leper. Now surely a leper can't be near the King and shouldn't be able to fight in anyone's battle, but he has done so much for the people. Why would you even add this information to the scripture? Considering the fact that the Bible gives us all things necessary to

LIFE and GODLINESS, I believe this was written for us to see ourselves in someone else's story.

No one ever verbally asked any of us to be perfect, but it is an unspoken expectation we feel the pressure to live up to. Can I say something and not be labeled a heretic? God never expects us to be perfect in our sense of the word being without flaws.

Let me explain.

In creation, when God made everything over again (that's for another day), even though he made it, the Bible says everything he saw was 'good' and even after he created man he said he was 'very good'. A flawless life makes Calvary unnecessary, but here is the celebration part.

James 1:2-4 says, *Consider it pure joy, my brothers and sisters, whenever you face trials of many kinds, 3because you know that the testing of your faith produces perseverance. 4Let perseverance finish its work so that you may be mature and complete, not lacking anything.*

When you realize perfection is about maturing more than perfection, I hope your chest went down a tad bit because a life without flaws was never the intended goal. Your imperfection does not disqualify you from being the captain of the ship, but it actually makes you more qualified than the inexperienced captain with no fight or grit to lead out an army.

Come out of hiding, show your disease, and expose your flaws so that you can be healed as you lead. You will do yourself a disservice if you try to maintain a false image of 'perfection'; and you become an imposter in your own mind. I know this sounds hard to do, and it is, but you will see that you are stronger and more confident when you're going through life healed and unashamed. Naaman went to the Man of God and got healed of his leprosy, (that's another post by itself), and left refreshed and renewed.

My prayer for you today is that you find a Man of God that you can trust, expose your wounds, be sober and willing, and receive your healing.

In what ways does this thought make me want to **RESTART**?

_____
_____
_____
_____
_____
_____
_____
_____
_____
_____

What steps am I willing to take today to **RESTART**?

1. _____
   _____
   _____

2. _____
   _____
   _____

3. _____
   _____
   _____

Day 8

It's Just The Season

> Galatians 6:9 NIV
>
> *Let us not become weary in doing good, for at the proper time we will reap a harvest if we do not give up.*

Some of the most crucial points in our lives start out with the ending of what would seem to be the toughest times in our lives. It is in those moments that we must try to figure out the purpose behind these night times. I'll tell you what the purpose is....experience. When you look at what's in front of you right now, it is really the door to your greatest time in life. When you look at the figures we admire today, whether it be spiritual or natural, you will see they didn't come through a life of green grass and lilies, but they came through a life of planting seeds and tending to the harvest. Even though sometimes they never saw a harvest, they learned to find somewhere else to plant and see what blossomed there. Just because the season you're in doesn't seem to be flourishing, it could be teaching you how to plant in the right direction and at the right time. Be patient.

This is a very tough mantra when our generation needs immediate results (microwave generation), but any good farmer will tell you that there are barren seasons and you must wait those out so that you can plant in the right season. Many of us are planting great seeds now and expecting a great harvest two weeks from now and then become disappointed in the ground. The problem is not the ground but it's the season. This is just to encourage everyone who reads this that your season for flourishing is soon to come. You just have to stand the process of growth and LEARN to WAIT on what you have planted to blossom. If you feel like quitting, DON'T! Keep learning everything you can at this point so you will cherish and properly tend to the harvest or manifestation of what is to come. In fact, get excited!

In what ways does this thought make me want to **RESTART**?

_____
_____
_____
_____
_____
_____
_____
_____
_____

What steps am I willing to take today to **RESTART**?

1. _____
   _____
   _____

2. _____
   _____
   _____

3. _____
   _____
   _____

Day 9

Pretty Hurts

> Genesis 1:3 NIV
> And God said, "Let there be light," and there was light.

We have been deceived into thinking that perfection means you have no flaws, and sadly, many of us have discounted where we are in life because we have concluded that perfection is unattainable. You are gladly mistaken. Perfection is a process of becoming whole.

When God created the heavens and the Earth, there was perfection because there was no one around to contaminate His creation. Most of us know the narrative of how an angel named Lucifer became prideful because of the applause and praise of those around him. He was extremely gifted and beautiful in his physical makeup. This speaks to us as creatives because we have a gift that many people envy and that is to create something out of nothing. Oh what a phenomenal gift! We have to hear something no one else hears, imagine what others cannot imagine, and turn it into a song or dance that no one has ever heard or even seen before. But I must warn you that the praise of people should make us feel good, but we must at the same time turn the attention and glory to God. But this was not his case.

If you read Isaiah 14:12-15, you will see an inside conversation Lucifer had with himself where he threatens to ascend into heaven and be on the same level as God.

> ^{12} How you have fallen from heaven,
> morning star, son of the dawn!
> You have been cast down to the earth,
> you who once laid low the nations!
> ^{13} You said in your heart,
> "I will ascend to the heavens;
> I will raise my throne
> above the stars of God;
> I will sit enthroned on the mount of assembly,
> on the utmost heights of Mount Zaphon.[a]
> ^{14} I will ascend above the tops of the clouds;
> I will make myself like the Most High."
> ^{15} But you are brought down to the realm of the dead,
> to the depths of the pit.

We see here that pride can lead to self-deception, and if you are not careful, your gift will be your demise. As a result, his pride has him thrown out of heaven and now it has thrown God's beautiful utopia into a chaotic mess. But God always has a plan to redeem His creation.

In our scripture today, there is a word used which is 'let'. In its original meaning, it means to call or present something forth that was already there. In other words, God does not create a new sun, moon, and vegetation but he does call back into place those things that were destroyed in chaos. But the best part of this story is how it relates to us as individuals because we have figured that what has happened to us and through us has kept us from perfection. You are absolutely right, but an even greater joy is to know that when God brought everything back into creation, He saw it and called it good. That being said, my prayer for you today is that you no longer beat yourself up over a standard God never set for you. Our job is to be good, which looks like living in a way that pleases God the best that you can. In the event that you miss the mark on your way to wholeness, he gives you grace to continue on the journey. God desires that we be whole and healed and this is obtainable through you staying focused on your future and not the mistakes of your past.

God is more concerned with your pursuit than your perfection!

In what ways does this thought make me want to **RESTART**?

_____
_____
_____
_____
_____
_____
_____
_____
_____

What steps am I willing to take today to **RESTART**?

1. _____
_____
_____

2. _____
_____
_____

3. _____
_____
_____

Day 10

Strong Desires

> Psalm 37:4 NIV
>
> *Take delight in the Lord, and he will give you the desires of your heart.*

If we know anything about David, he was much in tune with his emotions. You almost have to be careful which Psalm you read for your devotion because there are some Psalms where he is talking about the greatness of God and the next he is talking about his soul being anguished. One day the Earth is the Lord's, and the next day, God where are you? Needless to say, David sounds just like us.

In our scripture today, David is giving us a comparison between those who follow God and those who do not. Do not be envious of those who do wrong because their reward is instability and demise. But the key points here are to trust in God, do good, and cultivate faithfulness. The reward is given when we delight ourselves in Him. He gives us the desires of our heart. This can be good and bad because we must evaluate the desires of our heart. Are our desires God-centered? Are our desires selfish? Are our desires according to God's will for our lives? Think about it. If God gave you everything you desired, would you still be in His will? Well, the key to this verse is that you must delight yourself in God, and if you do this sincerely and diligently, eventually your desires become what he desires for you. This leads into a conversation about the Holy Spirit which Romans tells us makes intercession on our behalf when we do not know what to say. There can be times when we are making decisions and praying God's blessing on something that He doesn't desire for us, but when we are through, the Holy Spirit has to come in and intercept something that could be detrimental to your life.

My prayer for you today is that you will learn to delight yourself in God. Ask God to place His desires on you so that your decisions are centered around what God wants for you. It is in His word. Here are a few examples.

> Psalm 51:6 NIV
>
> Yet you desired faithfulness even in the womb; you taught me wisdom in that secret place.
>
> Jeremiah 29:11 NIV
>
> For I know the plans I have for you," declares the Lord, "plans to prosper you and not to harm you, plans to give you hope and a future.
>
> Matthew 10:29-31 NIV
>
> [29] Are not two sparrows sold for a penny? Yet not one of them will fall to the ground outside your Father's care.[a] [30] And even the very hairs of your head are all numbered. [31] So don't be afraid; you are worth more than many sparrows.
>
> Joshua 1:9 NIV
>
> Have I not commanded you? Be strong and courageous. Do not be afraid; do not be discouraged, for the Lord your God will be with you wherever you go."

In what ways does this thought make me want to **RESTART**?

What steps am I willing to take today to **RESTART**?

1.

2.

3.

Day 11

Arrogant Worship

> 1 Samuel 15:22 NIV
>
> But Samuel replied:
> "Does the Lord delight in burnt offerings and sacrifices
> as much as in obeying the Lord?
> To obey is better than sacrifice,
> and to heed is better than the fat of rams.

We are amongst some of the most talented minstrels and ministry gifts in history. We see the expansion of technology in worship and the production has been on the same level as some of the world's biggest stages. But in the midst of all of this expansion outwardly, we must never compromise our inward expansion.

There is something that is required of those who want to experience the fullness of God and that is a sacrifice. Now don't skip today's lesson because this is the most challenging day so far, but it's the most eye-opening. There are so many gifted individuals who have yet to surrender all that God has required of them. Therefore, as in our scripture, while we are 'worshipping', those who are listening can hear your flesh more than the spirit of God. Let's explore this deeper.

When praise and worship leaders are laying out the people they were called to lead, their flesh is still alive. When musicians have it out with their leaders over compensation, their flesh is still alive. When minstrels find ways to manipulate the atmosphere versus flowing with the spirit in the house, their flesh is very much alive. Now we have a form of godliness because it sounds like God, but we are denying the power which leads to pure worship and transformation.

In our scripture today, Saul has disobeyed the command of God and kept the things he liked and expected to offer them to God as a sacrifice. How many times have we tried to come into God's presence still holding on to relationships and mindsets that He told us to release? And for some reason, we have expected God to still accept what doesn't belong in His presence. When Saul is confronted by Samuel, his guilt (or delusion) speaks up quickly and says "I did everything God told me". Samuel the Prophet quickly says, 'why do I hear the sound of sheep bleating?' In other words, your disobedience is speaking louder than your worship. Then, we see the all-time favorite statement that obedience is better than sacrifice which communicates to us that God desires the worship he wants and not what we want to give him.

My prayer for you today is that you evaluate what you have been offering to God against what he desires you to sacrifice to him. This will be challenging but it is beneficial. Are you able to worship God withholding nothing?

In what ways does this thought make me want to **RESTART**?

_____
_____
_____
_____
_____
_____
_____
_____
_____
_____

What steps am I willing to take today to **RESTART**?

1. _____
_____
_____

2. _____
_____
_____

3. _____
_____
_____

Day 12

You Know You're Tired

> Psalm 23:2 NIV
>
> *He makes me lie down in green pastures,*
> *he leads me beside quiet waters,*

I am definitely considered a workaholic, which I wear at times as a badge. I often forget the benefits of rest as a tool God uses to speak to us. Let's be honest, working is what brings us joy and if we are not busy, we feel unproductive. But this can change in a matter of minutes.

Your rest is not a sign of laziness. It is actually a sign of stability because you prioritize your mental clarity over your need to feel busy. We are always given things to do. Therefore, we claim we are burned out, but tasks without systems lead to burnout. There is nothing wrong with being busy, but if you're going and going without proper rest scheduled, you will burn out.

Burnout looks like not enjoying what you once were passionate about because your passion turns into an obligation. You no longer enjoy ministry because you are operating on autopilot, and it shows in your output quality. This is no fun.

Once you get to this place, you read this scripture differently. We usually read this scripture in its poetic soft tone, but David says 'he MAKES me lie down in green pastures'. What this says to us is that if you do not take time to rest to be refreshed by God, He will make you lie down. This is when your body shuts down, which I have been guilty of ignoring. This is when you can't think straight to learn material. This is when you are now late for ministry because once you finally get to sleep your body takes over and all of a sudden, your comforter holds you hostage. But this does not have to be the case.

My prayer for you today is that you will train yourself to schedule times of rest that include sleep but also include time alone to hear from and get refreshed by God. Once you achieve this, you will see your mood much better. You will see your mind is clearer, and you will see your productivity back up to par.

In what ways does this thought make me want to **RESTART**?

_____
_____
_____
_____
_____
_____
_____
_____
_____
_____

What steps am I willing to take today to **RESTART**?

1. _____
_____
_____

2. _____
_____
_____

3. _____
_____
_____

Day 13

Eat Up

> Psalm 23:5 NIV
>
> *You prepare a table before me*
> *in the presence of my enemies.*
> *You anoint my head with oil;*
> *my cup overflows.*

We don't ever ask for enemies. Some enemies are inevitable. If you are anointed, you will have enemies. My Bishop even goes as far as to say that our warfare is an indication of our anointing. We did not ask to be great. We did not ask to be highly favored, and we sure did not ask to be anointed by God. If we did not ask for these things, we definitely never asked for the enemies attached to them. But here is the good news. Your enemy has already been defeated in your life.

David often uses agricultural references in his Psalms, and this is the perfect example. David speaks from his experience as a shepherd to compare his work to that of God who is our chief shepherd. Here's a proven fact. Sheep are dumb and always need their shepherd to save them.

In today's scripture, the farmer goes out while their sheep are asleep and clears out all of the poison that has been planted into the garden where the sheep graze from. This is helpful because the sheep can go and eat without the fear of being poisoned. What great news this is!

God, being our shepherd, knows what attacks the enemy has set up for us, but we can sometimes miss out on the distractions in our life that can turn deadly. But the God we serve never sleeps nor slumbers. Therefore, he never misses what can be waiting to take us out. This looks like bad motives, lustful temptations, and self-induced distractions. But while we are sleeping, literally or mentally, we can rest assured in the fact that no weapon formed against us shall be able to prosper because God has already cleared the way on our behalf.

My prayer for you today is that you worship God for keeping you safe when the enemy had a trap set up for you. You can go on through life without fear of poison!

In what ways does this thought make me want to **RESTART**?

_____
_____
_____
_____
_____
_____
_____
_____
_____

What steps am I willing to take today to **RESTART**?

1. _____
_____
_____

2. _____
_____
_____

3. _____
_____
_____

Day 14

Anoint My Head With Oil

One thing we learned yesterday was that sheep are dumb… ok that is my last time saying that. Oftentimes, we are compared to sheep to continue to remind us of our need for a shepherd. Our scripture is once again David using his profession as a Shepherd to relate to God being our Shepherd. I must be honest. This is one of my favorite scriptures to break down.

There are times in life when we as sheep constantly attempt to run from God's presence. We try to escape the green pastures, not realizing that there is safety in the green pastures. We see things outside the gate and want to run to those things, not knowing whether they are good or not. In David's experience, his sheep would often get their heads stuck in the gate while trying to escape. The only remedy he knew was to use oil to put around their necks and back them out of the gate. This is where it gets good. Not only does he use the oil to help them escape but he also uses oil to heal them. Before you get up and run around, look at yourself and wonder how you made it out of so many 'gates' and still had the ability to worship God. This is because oil is not just for deliverance, but it is also for your healing. Even more than that, it is a reminder to you of the grace of God. Even though he knows there will be times you try to go through the 'gate' again, he fixed it so that you have enough oil that you can pull yourself out and not be bruised in the process. That's a good place to run around and shout, "Anoint me, Lord!"

My prayer for you today is that you will come into a greater appreciation of the grace of God knowing that he is there to pull you out of anything you get yourself into. He is there to heal you. He has also prepared you and given you the ability to pull yourself out of any stronghold.

In what ways does this thought make me want to **RESTART**?

What steps am I willing to take today to **RESTART**?

1.

2.

3.

Day 15

The Right King

> Mark 3:1-6 NIV
>
> Another time Jesus went into the synagogue, and a man with a shriveled hand was there. ² Some of them were looking for a reason to accuse Jesus, so they watched him closely to see if he would heal him on the Sabbath. ³ Jesus said to the man with the shriveled hand, "Stand up in front of everyone."
>
> ⁴ Then Jesus asked them, "Which is lawful on the Sabbath: to do good or to do evil, to save life or to kill?" But they remained silent.
>
> ⁵ He looked around at them in anger and, deeply distressed at their stubborn hearts, said to the man, "Stretch out your hand." He stretched it out, and his hand was completely restored. ⁶ Then the Pharisees went out and began to plot with the Herodians how they might kill Jesus.

Everyone has something they are embarrassed about. Some would be considered worse than others. No matter how bad you think it is, we all have something we hope no one ever finds out about. There is hope for anyone who is willing to do one thing, expose it.

In our scripture today, there is a man that history tells us was working to build the temple in Jerusalem. Long story short, he was punished with all of the other Jewish workers for working on the Sabbath. As a result, amongst other punishments to his wife and children, his right hand was crushed. Due to this, he was forced to become a beggar and for 15 years never allowed to make eye contact with anyone. The king would come by and declare what was called "The Stone Mason's Disallowance". This read that his hand would never be healed. His sins would never be forgiven, and this is what God does to those who disobey him.

Serving should never be a traumatic situation, but unfortunately, that is not all of our testimony. Some of us have been under harsh leadership that left us broken and crushed in our spirit. One day while this man is sitting outside the temple, the right King comes into town and calls him out. Jesus, in front of everyone, requests that he expose his withered hand to him. At this point, he has the choice to keep his weakness hidden or expose it to be healed. He makes the right choice and stretches out his withered hand and Jesus restores his hand as if it was never crushed.

Today, even with no one around you, expose to God the areas you need him to heal. I heard a preacher say a long time ago, if you can stand to declare your weakness, God will stand to declare his power. Be healed today!

In what ways does this thought make me want to **RESTART**?

_____
_____
_____
_____
_____
_____
_____
_____
_____

What steps am I willing to take today to **RESTART**?

1. _____
_____
_____

2. _____
_____
_____

3. _____
_____
_____

Day 16

Waiting On God

> Psalm 130: 5-6 NIV
>
> I wait for the Lord, my whole being waits, and in his word I put my hope.
> I wait for the Lord more than watchmen wait for the morning, more than watchmen wait for the morning.

If there is one thing we don't like to do, it is to wait. For some reason, over and over again, God instructs us to wait on Him. This is frustrating because waiting works against our rushed timeline of when we want God to do things for us. We would love to pray and get an answer or solution right away, or is that just me? But unfortunately, God does not work that way and it is actually for our benefit.

While waiting on God, we are open to receiving instructions from him, encouraging words from him, and even seeing results done by him. While waiting on God, we receive so much clarity. Fun Fact: we don't have to be anxious over the things we often let trouble us. When he says in **1 Peter 5: 7** to ***cast all your cares on him, because he cares for you***, the word 'cares' is originally translated as anxiety. So, in actuality, he is saying that you should cast all of your anxiety on God because he is willing and able to fix what is worrying you. Make yourself aware of the fact that God cares for you which is sometimes uncomfortable. Please understand that he will make you wait for things you will cherish later on.

My prayer for you today is that you will learn to cast your anxiety on God and know that he will give you the strength you need to endure while he turns your situation around.

In what ways does this thought make me want to **RESTART**?

_____
_____
_____
_____
_____
_____
_____
_____
_____
_____

What steps am I willing to take today to **RESTART**?

1. _____
   _____
   _____

2. _____
   _____
   _____

3. _____
   _____
   _____

Day 17

Strength For The Journey

> 1 Kings 19:5-18 NIV
>
> 5 Then he lay down under the bush and fell asleep. All at once an angel touched him and said, "Get up and eat." 6 He looked around, and there by his head was some bread baked over hot coals, and a jar of water. He ate and drank and then lay down again.
>
> 7 The angel of the Lord came back a second time and touched him and said, "Get up and eat, for the journey is too much for you." 8 So he got up and ate and drank. Strengthened by that food, he traveled forty days and forty nights until he reached Horeb, the mountain of God. 9 There he went into a cave and spent the night.
>
> And the word of the Lord came to him: "What are you doing here, Elijah?"
>
> 10 He replied, "I have been very zealous for the LordGod Almighty. The Israelites have rejected your covenant, torn down your altars, and put your prophets to death with the sword. I am the only one left, and now they are trying to kill me too."
>
> 11 The Lord said, "Go out and stand on the mountain in the presence of the Lord, for the Lord is about to pass by."
>
> Then a great and powerful wind tore the mountains apart and shattered the rocks before the Lord, but the Lord was not in the wind. After the wind there was an earthquake, but the Lord was not in the earthquake.12 After the earthquake came a fire, but the Lord was not in the fire. And after the fire came a gentle whisper.13 When Elijah heard it, he pulled his cloak over his faceand went out and stood at the mouth of the cave.
>
> Then a voice said to him, "What are you doing here, Elijah?"

> 14 He replied, "I have been very zealous for the Lord God Almighty. The Israelites have rejected your covenant, torn down your altars, and put your prophets to death with the sword. I am the only one left, and now they are trying to kill me too."
>
> 15 The Lord said to him, "Go back the way you came, and go to the Desert of Damascus. When you get there, anoint Hazael king over Aram. 16 Also, anoint Jehu son of Nimshi king over Israel, and anoint Elisha son of Shaphat from Abel Meholah to succeed you as prophet. 17 Jehu will put to death any who escape the sword of Hazael, and Elisha will put to death any who escape the sword of Jehu. 18 Yet I reserve seven thousand in Israel—all whose knees have not bowed down to Baal and whose mouths have not kissed him."

Today is the day you remove all obstacles from your path, and the first obstacle is fear. Have you realized that most of your dreams have not been accomplished not because you did not know what to do but because you were fearful of the outcome? Or were you afraid of how you saw it turn out for others before you? No more will this be your obstacle.

In today's scripture, the Master Prophet Elijah experienced one of his greatest victories in single-handedly defeating 450 prophets of Baal, and now Jezebel (we will talk about her another day) is threatening to take his life. From this, he runs and hides under a tree and asks God to take his life before she does. What is it to be so anointed and used by God so mightily only to end up not desiring to live because of fear? We have all been there before - maybe not to the point of death, but to the point of quitting ministry altogether. However, something amazing happens. God reminds him of why he is here.

The angel gives him a set of instructions that I want to give to you today to move past fear. The first instruction is the get up from the tree. Get up from the place you find yourself hiding. Next, the angel tells him to eat and gain strength from your warfare so that you have strength for the next battle. Interestingly enough, the angel then tells him to go back to sleep. I know we all like that part but that is so that you can once again gain strength for what's to come. Next, it's time to eat again to be well prepared for the journey God is about to send him on. Lastly, God encourages him that he can no longer stay under the tree because he has to go and anoint Jehu, Hazel, and Elisha. What does this mean for you today?

My prayer for you today is that you choose to move past any fears you have about your future because of past experiences. People are waiting to receive what God has given you and the longer you stay in fear, the longer you keep yourself from impacting those that God has called you to be a blessing to.

In what ways does this thought make me want to **RESTART**?

_____
_____
_____
_____
_____
_____
_____
_____
_____
_____

What steps am I willing to take today to **RESTART**?

1. _____
   _____
   _____

2. _____
   _____
   _____

3. _____
   _____
   _____

Day 18

Walk By Faith

> John 9:7-11 NIV
>
> ⁷ "Go," he told him, "wash in the Pool of Siloam" (this word means "Sent"). So the man went and washed, and came home seeing.
> ⁸ His neighbors and those who had formerly seen him begging asked, "Isn't this the same man who used to sit and beg?" ⁹ Some claimed that he was.
> Others said, "No, he only looks like him."
> But he himself insisted, "I am the man."
> ¹⁰ "How then were your eyes opened?" they asked.
> ¹¹ He replied, "The man they call Jesus made some mud and put it on my eyes. He told me to go to Siloam and wash. So I went and washed, and then I could see."

Moving by faith is already a daunting task but imagine doing it without physical sight. Well, this is the basis of our text. Here is a man who is blind and looking for God to heal his sight, but instead of God just healing him, he tells him to go and wash his eyes out in the pool of Siloam. Now I don't mind obeying God, but there is another measure of faith required to go where he tells me without being able to see where I am going. You do the math.

Could this be the way God desires to stretch your faith, in that he will command you to do something that is almost humanly impossible? If you can trust God enough to make the move, you can experience another level of his work in your life. Here is the celebration. God is so calculated that he orchestrates the miracle in a way that even the steps he tells you to take are supposed to turn out in your favor. It's your responsibility to walk by faith, and not by what you can see with your physical eyes. Even if you don't understand what he is asking you to do, just trust that your steps are calculated by God.

My prayer today is that you will not be afraid to step out in faith, do what seems crazy to you, and see what great things God will do for, to, and through you.

In what ways does this thought make me want to **RESTART**?

_____
_____
_____
_____
_____
_____
_____
_____
_____
_____

What steps am I willing to take today to **RESTART**?

1. _____
   _____
   _____

2. _____
   _____
   _____

3. _____
   _____
   _____

Day 19

It's Only A Matter Of Time

> Luke 1:39-45 NIV
>
> [39] At that time Mary got ready and hurried to a town in the hill country of Judea, [40] where she entered Zechariah's home and greeted Elizabeth. [41] When Elizabeth heard Mary's greeting, the baby leaped in her womb, and Elizabeth was filled with the Holy Spirit. [42] In a loud voice she exclaimed: "Blessed are you among women, and blessed is the child you will bear! [43] But why am I so favored, that the mother of my Lord should come to me? [44] As soon as the sound of your greeting reached my ears, the baby in my womb leaped for joy. [45] Blessed is she who has believed that the Lord would fulfill his promises to her!"

When we consider the ways of the world now, it can be quite discouraging through our natural eyes, but if we ever look out at our world through the eyes of God, we will see that things are just about to get better. In Luke Chapter 21, Jesus is telling his followers about the signs of the last day. He's talking about earthquakes, famines, and persecution of the church, but he says when these things begin to happen…look up for your redemption draweth nigh. I come to tell somebody that when things in your life start looking crazy and in disarray, don't get mad. Get glad because that's just God's way of getting you ready for what's coming next and what's coming next looks a whole lot better than what you're looking at right now.

In today's scripture, we meet Mary, the mother of Jesus, who has just been told that her timeline for starting her family has just been rearranged by the Holy Spirit. God then sends her over to her cousin Elizabeth's house for a confirmation she didn't know she needed. She gets to Elizabeth and as soon as Mary greets her, the baby that was not moving in her womb leaped in her womb and she makes a declaration to Mary. To cut to our encouragement today, she tells her that there shall be a performance of the things that God spoke to her.

My prayer for you today is that you don't allow what seems like a resetting of your plans to make you think God has changed his mind about what he promised you. Better yet, get excited because it is only a matter of time before God does what he originally desired to do in your life. Time is not working against you, but time is on your side.

In what ways does this thought make me want to **RESTART**?

_____
_____
_____
_____
_____
_____
_____
_____
_____
_____

What steps am I willing to take today to **RESTART**?

1. _____
   _____
   _____

2. _____
   _____
   _____

3. _____
   _____
   _____

Day 20

A Reason To Continue

> *Jeremiah 29:11 NIV*
>
> *For I know the plans I have for you," declares the Lord, "plans to prosper you and not to harm you, plans to give you hope and a future.*

The children of Israel were rather rebellious. Because God is our father, every now and then he has to place them in punishment for them to learn a lesson. Notice I said to learn a lesson because we often think the punishment of God is to our demise not realizing that he only chastises those whom he loves. Therefore, anytime you feel conviction, it's a sign that God loves you.

Well, this is the situation around our scripture today. Israel is being put into bondage in Babylon because of their disobedience to God, but he does something to affirm his love for them in the midst of this bondage. First, he gives them strategies on how to grow their families and go into business while still in bondage. Secondly, he lets them know that this bondage is a part of the plan that he has for them.

My prayer for you today is that you will rethink your conviction from a negative feeling of shame to a sign that no matter what mistakes you make, God is not standing by waiting to punish you but better yet, he is standing by waiting to get you focused on his plan for your life.

In what ways does this thought make me want to **RESTART**?

_____
_____
_____
_____
_____
_____
_____
_____

What steps am I willing to take today to **RESTART**?

1. _____
_____
_____

2. _____
_____
_____

3. _____
_____
_____

Day 21

A New Man

1 Samuel 10 NIV

Then Samuel took a flask of olive oil and poured it on Saul's head and kissed him, saying, "Has not the Lord anointed you ruler over his inheritance?[a] 2 When you leave me today, you will meet two men near Rachel's tomb, at Zelzah on the border of Benjamin. They will say to you, 'The donkeys you set out to look for have been found. And now your father has stopped thinking about them and is worried about you. He is asking, "What shall I do about my son?"'

3 "Then you will go on from there until you reach the great tree of Tabor. Three men going up to worship God at Bethel will meet you there. One will be carrying three young goats, another three loaves of bread, and another a skin of wine. 4 They will greet you and offer you two loaves of bread, which you will accept from them.

5 "After that you will go to Gibeah of God, where there is a Philistine outpost. As you approach the town, you will meet a procession of prophets coming down from the high place with lyres, timbrels, pipes and harpsbeing played before them, and they will be prophesying. 6 The Spirit of the Lord will come powerfully upon you, and you will prophesy with them; and you will be changed into a different person. 7 Once these signs are fulfilled, do whatever your hand finds to do, for God is with you.

8 "Go down ahead of me to Gilgal. I will surely come down to you to sacrifice burnt offerings and fellowship offerings, but you must wait seven days until I come to you and tell you what you are to do."

9 As Saul turned to leave Samuel, God changed Saul's heart, and all these signs were fulfilled that day.10 When he and his servant arrived at Gibeah, a procession of prophets met him; the Spirit of God came powerfully upon him, and he joined in their prophesying. 11 When all those who had formerly known him saw him prophesying with the prophets, they asked each other, "What is this that has happened to the son of Kish? Is Saul also among the prophets?"

12 A man who lived there answered, "And who is their father?" So it became a saying: "Is Saul also among the prophets?" 13 After Saul stopped prophesying, he went to the high place.

14 Now Saul's uncle asked him and his servant, "Where have you been?"

"Looking for the donkeys," he said. "But when we saw they were not to be found, we went to Samuel."

15 Saul's uncle said, "Tell me what Samuel said to you."

16 Saul replied, "He assured us that the donkeys had been found." But he did not tell his uncle what Samuel had said about the kingship.

17 Samuel summoned the people of Israel to the Lord at Mizpah 18 and said to them, "This is what the Lord, the God of Israel, says: 'I brought Israel up out of Egypt, and I delivered you from the power of Egypt and all the kingdoms that oppressed you.' 19 But you have now rejected your God, who saves you out of all your disasters and calamities. And you have said, 'No, appoint a king over us.' So now present yourselves before the Lord by your tribes and clans."

20 When Samuel had all Israel come forward by tribes, the tribe of Benjamin was taken by lot. 21 Then he brought forward the tribe of Benjamin, clan by clan, and Matri's clan was taken. Finally Saul son of Kish was taken. But when they looked for him, he was not to be found. 22 So they inquired further of the Lord, "Has the man come here yet?"

And the Lord said, "Yes, he has hidden himself among the supplies."

23 They ran and brought him out, and as he stood among the people he was a head taller than any of the others. 24 Samuel said to all the people, "Do you see the man the Lord has chosen? There is no one like him among all the people."

Then the people shouted, "Long live the king!"

25 Samuel explained to the people the rights and duties of kingship. He wrote them down on a scroll and deposited it before the Lord. Then Samuel dismissed the people to go to their own homes.

26 Saul also went to his home in Gibeah, accompanied by valiant men whose hearts God had touched. 27 But some scoundrels said, "How can this fellow save us?" They despised him and brought him no gifts. But Saul kept silent.

Today is the day you shake off any self-doubt and walk into your God-given identity.

Easier said than done you say? Let me explain how this can happen. Put people in your life that are going where you are going as well.

In our scripture today, Saul has just been told that he is going to be King over Israel and immediately, like us, he reaches into his arsenal and loads up his excuses as to why God could not be talking about him. He goes down the list of how he is from the smallest family of the smallest tribe. In other words, he is not prestigious enough to be the King, but little does he know that God often uses what man would consider the unqualified to do great things for his kingdom. So, the same way God gave Moses, Aaron, to help him - the same way he gave Ruth, Mordecai, to help her, he gave Saul a group of prophets. This is the group of individuals to give you a preview of what you were called to do. Here is the best part. Once Saul met these prophets, according to the word of Samuel, Saul began to do, in one day, what these men trained for years to accomplish.

My encouragement today is that God has already supplied you with the gift you need for your purpose in life. Your next step is to connect with people who will take you under their wing and give you an intensive on how to use what's on the inside of you.

In what ways does this thought make me want to **RESTART**?

_____
_____
_____
_____
_____
_____
_____
_____
_____

What steps am I willing to take today to **RESTART**?

1. _____
_____
_____

2. _____
_____
_____

3. _____
_____
_____

Day 22

Anything Is Possible

> Philippians 4:13 NIV
> I can do all this through him who gives me strength.

A lot of our fear comes from a lack of knowledge, and this has been the cause of some setbacks that we have experienced in life. Maybe no one told you how truly gifted you are, how anointed you are, or how intelligent you are. Imagine what you could have accomplished with this in your mind. This is where Paul relates to us.

As a believer, you have the spirit and image of God indwelling inside of you, and with this comes his limitless ability. This is good to know because not only are we able to move in the spirit, but we are able to operate in our natural world without limits. Be free from a false sense of weakness and inferiority amongst other people on your circle. If we believe that according to scripture the same spirit that raised Jesus has also quickened our mortal body, then who are we to walk around as if we have no power in the Earth? When Paul says 'all' he is using an absolute term. This means nothing can be added to it or taken away from it. My prayer for you is that you take the limits off of your mind, your creativity, and your execution because that's when you will experience the endless supply of God's power in your life.

Dream bigger. Work harder. Stretch yourself. You can do all things through Christ and only through Christ that strengthens you.

In what ways does this thought make me want to **RESTART**?

_____

_____

_____

_____

_____

_____

_____

_____

_____

What steps am I willing to take today to **RESTART**?

1. _____

_____

_____

2. _____

_____

_____

3. _____

_____

_____

Day 23

Are You Ready To Turn?

> 2 Chronicles 7:14 NIV
>
> *If my people, who are called by my name, will humble themselves and pray and seek my face and turn from their wicked ways, then I will hear from heaven, and I will forgive their sin and will heal their land.*

Since the beginning of time, God has always had requirements as to how he wants his people to live. We first see these in Leviticus which most of us have never attempted to read. I will save you the trouble and let you know that it is impossible for us to meet every requirement set for us. This is why we should be thankful that Jesus did not come to do away with the law, but he came to fulfill the law. This is why, even though the priest had to go before God once a year to make sacrifices for the sins of the people, Hebrews 10 tells us that he made the sacrifice once and for all. Therefore, we are not responsible for dying for the sins we commit from time to time. He does require something in response to his sacrifice: repentance.

This is not repentance in the way we think. The true definition of repentance is the act of turning away from something. In other words, he requires us to turn away from the sins we have been forgiven of. He tells us in Hebrews 12 to lay aside the sin and weight that easily besets us if we are going to run this race that is set before us. To the point of today's scripture, our act of humbling ourselves and turning from our sins will cause God to hear from heaven, forgive our sins, and ultimately heal our land. We have places in our lives that need restoration and healing, and God wants to do the work of healing those places.

My prayer for you today is that you make the hard decisions, have the hard conversations, and turn from some old habits for God to do his part and heal those places in your life that hold you back from your full potential in God.

In what ways does this thought make me want to **RESTART**?

_____
_____
_____
_____
_____
_____
_____
_____
_____

What steps am I willing to take today to **RESTART**?

1. _____
_____
_____

2. _____
_____
_____

3. _____
_____
_____

Day 24

Be Not Weary

> Galatians 6:9 NIV
>
> Let us not become weary in doing good, for at the proper time we will reap a harvest if we do not give up.

If we are not careful, we can fall into the trap of feeling as if what we do is not effective. We will begin to feel like we give so much to get so little in return and the pay doesn't match the productivity. My friend, this is the first stage of burnout. Beware when these thoughts start to fill your head.

What you do is meaningful, and it is making an impact on lives daily. Your service to God serves others and it serves you as well. Don't get disheartened when it seems you are being looked over. God sees your work. Not only does God see you but people are watching your life and taking notes. You may not get all of the rewards right now but there is a due date for your reward. Many greats have learned to serve in silence. This silence isn't limited to just them but the silence from those around them, knowing that one day the proper accolades will come.

We have a scripture that our volunteers read every Sunday in our morning huddle.

> Colossians 3:23-24 NASB95
>
> 23 Whatever you do, do your work heartily, as for the Lord rather than for men,
>
> 24 knowing that from the Lord you will receive the reward of the inheritance. It is the Lord Christ whom you serve. Only what you do for Christ will last.

In what ways does this thought make me want to **RESTART**?

_____
_____
_____
_____
_____
_____
_____
_____
_____

What steps am I willing to take today to **RESTART**?

1. _____
   _____
   _____

2. _____
   _____
   _____

3. _____
   _____
   _____

Day 25

Never Forget

> Lamentations 3: 21-23 NIV
>
> Yet this I call to mind and therefore I have hope:
> ²² Because of the Lord's great love we are not consumed, for his compassions never fail.
> ²³ They are new every morning; great is your faithfulness.

May we never lose our ability to remember, because our memory is what gives us hope for the future. When times get hard and it seems like God is 'distant', simply remembering his faithfulness in the past should remind you of how near and present he really is.

When you are low in your faith, remember all the times he brought you through before.

When you can't find a reason to smile, think about the times when you felt his love before. If we believe that he is the same yesterday, in your today, and in your future, then we must be encouraged that the God we serve is always near and is always present. That should give you hope in the fact that no matter what comes against you, God is faithful and committed to seeing you through.

Go through today knowing that you serve a faithful and ever-present God.

In what ways does this thought make me want to **RESTART**?

_____
_____
_____
_____
_____
_____
_____
_____
_____

What steps am I willing to take today to **RESTART**?

1. _____
   _____
   _____

2. _____
   _____
   _____

3. _____
   _____
   _____

Day 26

Your True Identity

> Judges 6:11-12 NIV
>
> The angel of the Lord came and sat down under the oak in Ophrah that belonged to Joash the Abiezrite, where his son Gideon was threshing wheat in a winepress to keep it from the Midianites. ¹²When the angel of the Lord appeared to Gideon, he said, "The Lord is with you, mighty warrior."

Be free from the labels you have allowed yourself to wear that have been placed on you by other individuals. Who you are in life is who God created you to be originally and that is the identity you should seek to fulfill. Today's scripture really hits home when you consider that the angel calls Gideon a valiant warrior while he is hiding and is fearful. You can somehow find out the truth about yourself when you are operating opposite of your identity. It takes being around people who are truth-speakers in your life. They will speak the truth to you that is sometimes hard to accept in the initial moment. Later, you will thank God for sending them your way.

Even though Gideon is not fully convinced throughout his story, he moves in confidence in the God who gave him this identity.

My prayer for you today is that you will ask God to keep those around you who will challenge you and allow you to operate, not fully convinced until you become fully convinced!

In what ways does this thought make me want to **RESTART**?

_____
_____
_____
_____
_____
_____
_____
_____
_____

What steps am I willing to take today to **RESTART**?

1. _____
   _____
   _____

2. _____
   _____
   _____

3. _____
   _____
   _____

Day 27

It Is You!

Esther 4:1-14 NIV

When Mordecai learned of all that had been done, he tore his clothes, put on sackcloth and ashes, and went out into the city, wailing loudly and bitterly. ² But he went only as far as the king's gate, because no one clothed in sackcloth was allowed to enter it. ³ In every province to which the edict and order of the king came, there was great mourning among the Jews, with fasting, weeping and wailing. Many lay in sackcloth and ashes.

⁴ When Esther's eunuchs and female attendants came and told her about Mordecai, she was in great distress. She sent clothes for him to put on instead of his sackcloth, but he would not accept them. ⁵ Then Esther summoned Hathak, one of the king's eunuchs assigned to attend her, and ordered him to find out what was troubling Mordecai and why.

⁶ So Hathak went out to Mordecai in the open square of the city in front of the king's gate. ⁷ Mordecai told him everything that had happened to him, including the exact amount of money Haman had promised to pay into the royal treasury for the destruction of the Jews. ⁸ He also gave him a copy of the text of the edict for their annihilation, which had been published in Susa, to show to Esther and explain it to her, and he told him to instruct her to go into the king's presence to beg for mercy and plead with him for her people.

⁹ Hathak went back and reported to Esther what Mordecai had said. ¹⁰ Then she instructed him to say to Mordecai, ¹¹ "All the king's officials and the people of the royal provinces know that for any man or woman who approaches the king in the inner court without being summoned the king has but one law: that they be put to death unless the king extends the gold scepterto them and spares their lives. But thirty days have passed since I was called to go to the king."

> [12] When Esther's words were reported to Mordecai, [13] he sent back this answer: "Do not think that because you are in the king's house you alone of all the Jews will escape. [14] For if you remain silent at this time, relief and deliverance for the Jews will arise from another place, but you and your father's family will perish. And who knows but that you have come to your royal position for such a time as this?"

You have survived some of the worst things you could have experienced. You have overcome the toughest of situations. You have lived to tell so many stories that can minister to others. All of this is for nothing if you never seek to realize the purpose for all of these victories. I once heard Nick Cannon say 'God gives his toughest battles to his strongest warriors'. This could not be truer, but there is a chance you can miss out on your purpose in life.

In today's scripture, Esther finds out her purpose, and per usual, fear begins to rise on the inside of her. You may have a purpose that scared you because it seems to be too great for you to accomplish, but I want to encourage you the way Mordecai, her guardian cousin, does. God has a plan for his people, and he has chosen you to fulfill that plan. If you decide not to because of fear, he will use someone else. Please consider that he chose you for this particular moment in history to make a difference in the world. You are chosen. You are God-picked. You are God-sent.

In what ways does this thought make me want to **RESTART**?

_____
_____
_____
_____
_____
_____
_____
_____
_____

What steps am I willing to take today to **RESTART**?

1. _____
   _____
   _____

2. _____
   _____
   _____

3. _____
   _____
   _____

Day 28

Unending Worship

> Revelation 4:8 NIV
>
> Each of the four living creatures had six wings and was covered with eyes all around, even under its wings. Day and night they never stop saying:
>
> "'Holy, holy, holy
>
> is the Lord God Almighty,'[a]
>
> who was, and is, and is to come."

What is your song to God? What comes to mind when you think of God that causes you to worship him? This is what creates endless worship: a constant state of gratitude towards God. We have so much to be grateful for and we should be without a loss for words when we consider how great our God is. Use this framework to create your unending worship of God.

In today's scripture, John is giving us insight into the visions that God gave him of the worship taking place in Heaven. In this particular case, imagine hearing angels singing for days but realizing they have been singing the same song the whole time.

"Holy, holy, holy is the Lord God, the Almighty,

who was and who is and who is to come."

There was no need to change their song because there is no part of this song that changes with who God is.

My prayer for you today is that you find your song that never ends about God, and never let it change. Get caught up in his presence and dwell there.

In what ways does this thought make me want to **RESTART**?

_____
_____
_____
_____
_____
_____
_____
_____
_____

What steps am I willing to take today to **RESTART**?

1. _____
_____
_____

2. _____
_____
_____

3. _____
_____
_____

Day 29

Why Come Down?

> Nehemiah 6:1-3 NIV
>
> When word came to Sanballat, Tobiah, Geshem the Arab and the rest of our enemies that I had rebuilt the wall and not a gap was left in it—though up to that time I had not set the doors in the gates— 2 Sanballat and Geshem sent me this message: "Come, let us meet together in one of the villages[a] on the plain of Ono."
> But they were scheming to harm me; 3 so I sent messengers to them with this reply: "I am carrying on a great project and cannot go down. Why should the work stop while I leave it and go down to you?"

Stay focused on your purpose, even when it seems as if you lack support from those who should be supporting you. There will be times when you have to be your greatest supporter, your own cheerleader, and your own coach. Needless to say, you must be secure in who you are before you can expect it from anyone else. Nehemiah is a great example of this.

Long story short, Nehemiah is on a mission to rebuild the walls of a ruined Jerusalem after receiving news that the city was in ruins. While he was working on this mission, his friends started taunting him and trying to discourage him because of the stagnation in their lives. Instead of accepting the discouragement, he gives the perfect response to those who are trying to distract him in any season of his life. He tells them, he will not come down from the wall to their level because he is about a good work.

Let this be your response when people try to talk you down from what you are working on! Don't come down from what God has given you to accomplish!

In what ways does this thought make me want to **RESTART**?

_____
_____
_____
_____
_____
_____
_____
_____

What steps am I willing to take today to **RESTART**?

1. _____
_____
_____

2. _____
_____
_____

3. _____
_____
_____

Day 30

Make This A Habit

> Psalm 1:1-3 NIV
>
> Blessed is the one who does not walk in step with the wicked or stand in the way that sinners take
> or sit in the company of mockers,
> ² but whose delight is in the law of the Lord, and who meditates on his law day and night.
> ³ That person is like a tree planted by streams of water, which yields its fruit in season and whose leaf does not wither — whatever they do prospers.

This devotional represents a framework for your everlasting communion with God. This is necessary to sustain your relationship with God. Whether you are reading this as a musician, singer, or just someone who wants to take your relationship with God to new heights, let this become something you continue to do daily. You will find in today's scripture the opening to the book of Psalms where David gives the characteristics of a man building his relationship with God.

For the sake of the brevity of our entries, let's look at verse 2. The best way to grow your relationship with God is to find ways to delight yourself in him. David's way was to meditate on his law day and night but let's be realistic. We have 9-5's and other obligations but yet, this is still possible. Having a devotional is great, but having a scripture you read in the morning and think about throughout your day keeps you in constant gratitude to God.

Try this out and see how much better your days become because there is no greater feeling than being in communion with the God who wants to talk to you day and night.

In what ways does this thought make me want to **RESTART**?

_____
_____
_____
_____
_____
_____
_____
_____
_____

What steps am I willing to take today to **RESTART**?

1. _____
_____
_____

2. _____
_____
_____

3. _____
_____
_____

Resources

Holy Bible, New International Version (NIV)

Holy Bible, New American Standard Bible 1995 (NASB95)

About The Author

Bruce Johnson, Jr.

Known for his revelatory yet practical teaching style, Bruce Johnson, Jr's love for the word and things of God is always evident. Growing up, he was always inspired by his mother's love for writing and his father's passion for studying the word of God. As a result, Bruce took this inspiration and wrote songs, blogs, and now finally his first devotional. He is the loving husband of Mrs. Soraya Johnson and the proud father of Mckenzie Solange and Averi Rose.

Bruce is the Pastor of The Ramp Church Richmond, affectionately known as 'The Upper Room Experience". His passion for seeing the people of God walk into a true awareness of the life God designed for them is the push behind his preaching, music, and his writings.

Bruce's motto in ministry is to preach/teach until all have heard.

www.ingramcontent.com/pod-product-compliance
Lightning Source LLC
LaVergne TN
LVHW061039070526
838201LV00073B/5107